TULSA CITY-COUNTY LI'

BKMOS

Y0-DJP-290

Tap It!

LEVEL 1

/a/t/
/p/i/

DEC●DABLES
BY jump!

Teaching Tips

Pink Level 1

This book focuses on the phonemes **/a/t/p/i/**.

Before Reading
- Discuss the title. Ask readers what they think the book will be about.
- Sound out the words on page 3 together.

Read the Book
- Ask readers to use a finger to follow along with each word as it is read.
- Encourage readers to break down unfamiliar words into units of sound. Then, ask them to string the sounds together to create the words.
- Urge readers to point out when the focused phonics phonemes appear in the text.

After Reading
- Encourage children to reread the book independently or with a friend.
- Guide readers through the phonics exercises at the end of the book.

© 2024 Booklife Publishing
This edition is published by arrangement with Booklife Publishing.

North American adaptations © 2024 Jump!
5357 Penn Avenue South
Minneapolis, MN 55419
www.jumplibrary.com

Decodables by Jump! are published by Jump! Library.
All rights reserved. No part of this book may be reproduced in any form without written permission from the publisher.

Library of Congress Cataloging-in-Publication Data is available at www.loc.gov or upon request from the publisher.

ISBN: 979-8-88524-703-0 (hardcover)
ISBN: 979-8-88524-704-7 (paperback)
ISBN: 979-8-88524-705-4 (ebook)

Photo Credits

Images are courtesy of Shutterstock.com. With thanks to Getty Images, Thinkstock Photo and iStockphoto. Cover - Asier Romer, Gaidamashchuk, Shanvood, Natalia Sheinkin, trucic. Page 4 – Milosz Aniol. Page 5 – Flashon Studio. Page 6 – Mister-john. Page 7 – Lorraine Swanson. Page 8 – AlenKadr. Page 9 – Lorraine Swanson. Page 10 – Nagy-Bagoly Arpad. Page 11 – Ilike. Page 15 – Shutterstock.

Can you find these words in the book?

it

tap

Tap it!

Tap tap tap.

Tap it!

Tap tap tap.

Tap it!

Tap tap tap.

Tap it!

Tap tap tap!

Can you say these sounds and draw them with your finger?

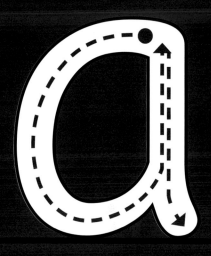

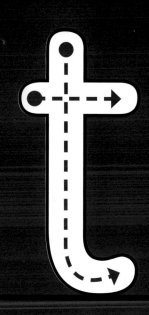

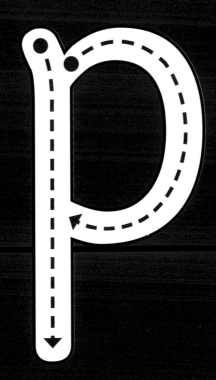

Using the Letter Bank, trace the missing letter into each word.

t_p

i_

_it

Letter Bank

t   a   p

What other words do you know
with the letters /a/, /t/, /p/, or /i/?

pit

cat

map

Practice reading the book again:

Tap it!

Tap tap tap.

Tap it!

Tap tap tap.

Tap it!

Tap tap tap.

Tap it!

Tap tap tap!

MYcAM